A Hand for Spelling
Activity Book 3

by
Charles Cripps and Janet Ede
with illustrations and design by
Bryony Jacklin

A Hand for Spelling Activity Book 3
Ref. LD683
ISBN 1 85503 155 8

© Living and Learning (Cambridge) Ltd. 1992
© Text Charles Cripps and Janet Ede
© Illustrations Bryony Jacklin

   Duke Street, Wisbech, Cambs PE13 2AE

Printed in Great Britain by
Ebenezer Baylis Ltd, Worcester

The Authors

Charles Cripps is a tutor at the Cambridge Institute of Education and runs courses for teachers of children with learning difficulties, with particular reference to communication skills, in mainstream schools.

He lectures nationally and internationally on the teaching of spelling and has many publications including *An Eye for Spelling*, ESM; co-author with Janet Ede of *Hands on Spelling*, ESM; *Stile Spelling Programme*, LDA; *Stile Early Spelling Cards*, LDA and co-author with Robin Cox of *Joining the ABC*.

His recent research was investigating the link between handwriting and how the teaching of joined writing on school entry influences the catching of spelling. *A Hand for Spelling* has come out of this research.

Janet Ede was until recently Senior Lecturer in English and Warden of the Language and Reading Centre, Derbyshire College of Higher Education (formerly Matlock College of Higher Education).

Her main interests are concerned with children's use of language in both the primary and secondary sectors.

She was co-director of the Schools' Council Project 'Teaching Poetry 9-13'.

Contents

Activity Book 3 will support the work done in *A Hand for Spelling Book 3*. The pages in each book are matched according to letter patterns. Many of the activities are open-ended and it is for teachers to decide whether children should write out the entire sentence or simply fill in the missing words. The important aspect of the activities is encouraging children to 'look' at familiar letter patterns and then write these letters in a connected form. Writing these letter patterns and words from memory must be encouraged throughout.

Sheets 91 and 92 allow you to create your own worksheets, using your own word groups.

Introduction

Since the HMI Report, *Education 5-9* (1982), which found that there was a lack of systematic and regular practice in the teaching of handwriting, there has been a renewed interest in this area of the skill. Moreover, the National Curriculum has given us both the stages and guidance as to how the teaching of this skill can best be achieved.

As the non-statutory guidance states, children need to be able to write legibly and must learn to form their letters correctly. The suggestions in the non-statutory guidance for planning schemes of work are totally endorsed and supported within the programme *A Hand for Spelling* which encourages children to develop a legible hand by emphasising movement through the word.

This programme also argues that the attainment targets as outlined in the National Curriculum can best be met when teachers recognise the value of introducing children to joined writing from the beginning. Recent research strongly supports this view and shows that children who are introduced to joined writing quickly develop confidence and are able to write with speed and enthusiasm. Moreover, such free-flowing writing has a strong influence on the 'catching' of spelling.

Spelling is a hand–eye skill. Good spelling and good handwriting go together. Good spellers look carefully at words and it is through this visual familiarity that they learn the probability of certain letters occurring together before writing them in a well-formed legible style of handwriting.

There is considerable evidence to show that both the visual imagery needed for success at spelling and the kinaesthetic imagery needed for free-flowing handwriting can be taught, and it is logical that they should be taught together.

The programme *A Hand for Spelling* is based on the strong principle that free-flowing handwriting contributes to success in spelling. *Joining the ABC* (Cripps & Cox, 1989) LDA, presents in detail the rationale behind, and gives practical guidelines for using *A Hand for Spelling* and integrating joined writing into the school's spelling policy.

Structure of A Hand for Spelling

A Hand for Spelling consists of four books of photocopy masters designed for 5-11 year olds and older pupils with learning difficulties.

It follows on from the natural, free scribble movements which children make when they first hold a pencil. These are then harnessed into pattern work from which a 'running hand' will follow.

Book 1 develops the pre-writing skills and gives children practice in pencil control and fine motor movements, before introducing letter formation.

Books 2 - 4 give children the opportunity of looking at and writing words which contain the same letter pattern. It teaches them to join letters together as early as possible, without using lines. Lines are unnecessary for the development of movement and can inhibit natural flow.

Accompanying activity books support the skills introduced in each main book and provide further practice before moving on.

The words have been selected from the known writing vocabularies of children and are presented in the following age bands:

Book 2   Ages 5 - 7
Book 3   Ages 7 - 9
Book 4   Ages 9 - 11

Within each of these books the worksheets are presented alphabetically, not in order of difficulty.

The teacher can select worksheets that deal with the letter patterns most appropriate for the needs of the group or an individual child. Some worksheets may be needed on more than one occasion, and some words appear in more than one worksheet. This either because the letter pattern is repeated across the age ranges or that the words contain more than one particular letter pattern, for example, 'ere' 'the' or 'her' in 'there'.

It will also be noted that in each workbook there is a mixture of print and joined writing. Instructions which are for reading are in print, whilst the joined writing, which can also be read, provides the model for handwriting.

In *A Hand for Spelling* use is made of some capital letters, for example, 'I' and 'C', as in 'Christmas'. The style recommended for all capital letters is bold print and not joined to the lower case letter. The apostrophe 's' as in 'hasn't', 'wasn't' etc. is also used, hence the reason for its usage will need to be taught. It will also be noted that the letters 'g', 'j', 'y' and 'z' do not join. This is intentional as the fully looped letter can be difficult for young children. This style also encourages pen lifts which will be essential later on for writing with speed.

What is important is the movement through the word, so for words containing these letters the procedure is as follows:

● If the word begins with a 'g', 'j', 'y' or 'z', then it is formed as a single letter, with the following letter beginning from the position it was taught as a single flowing letter.

● If the letters 'g', 'j', 'y' or 'z' appear within the word, then they are joined to the preceding letter in the usual way but completed as a single letter. The following letter begins as described above.

Teaching Points

Spelling

- Encourage close visual inspection of words and ensure children compare their written effort to the one they have studied.

- Collect and talk about words containing common letter patterns.

- Look for words within words. Visual discrimination of word form is a crucial part of learning how words are structured.

- Encourage the 'Look–Cover–Write–Check' routine. Remember the important aspect of this routine is the writing from memory.

- Provide opportunities for children to write words in context as well as practise the letter patterns.

Handwriting

- A correct pencil grip is firm but relaxed. The writing implement should be held between the thumb and the first finger, resting against the middle finger.

- Ensure correct letter formation at all times. (See the following pages for letter formation for both right and left-handed children)

- Ensure correct posture with children sitting comfortably with feet flat on the floor with body upright but tilted slightly forward on a chair suited to the height of the table.

- Children should have good light in order to see what they are writing without eye strain.

- The paper position should be adjusted to suit right or left-handers, that is, find the writing position which is the most comfortable.

- Provision must be made for left-handed children. If these children are taught how to be left-handed then they can write as freely and legibly as right-handed children. Additional information regarding left-handed children can be found in *Joining the ABC*, LDA.

Develop the language of writing

The language of writing is also important as it enables children to verbalise their physical actions and to understand the language used in the writing experience.

- Teach and use letter names not sounds.

- Teach words such as top , bottom, up, down, round, over, back, letter, word, pattern, left, right, join, curved, straight, etc.

(Teachers may add to this list)

Letter formation for right-handed children

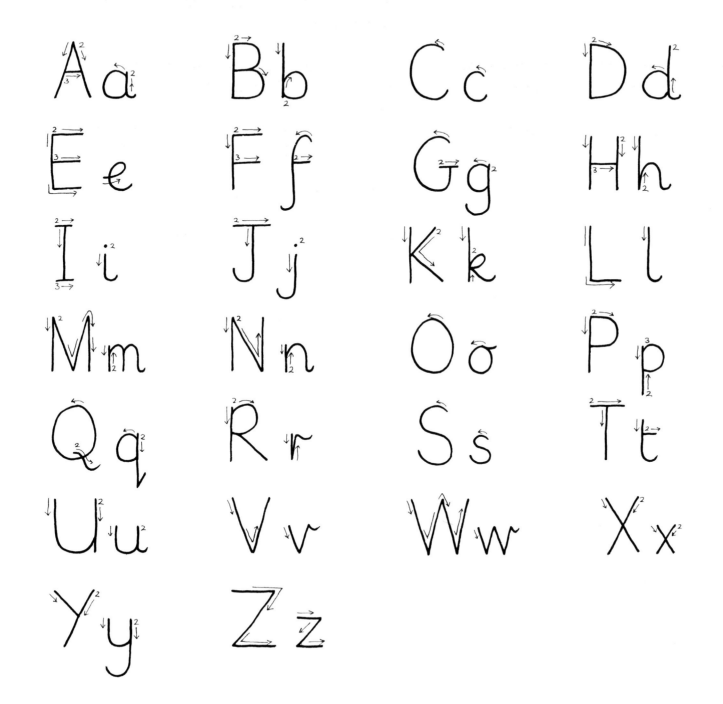

Letter formation for left-handed children

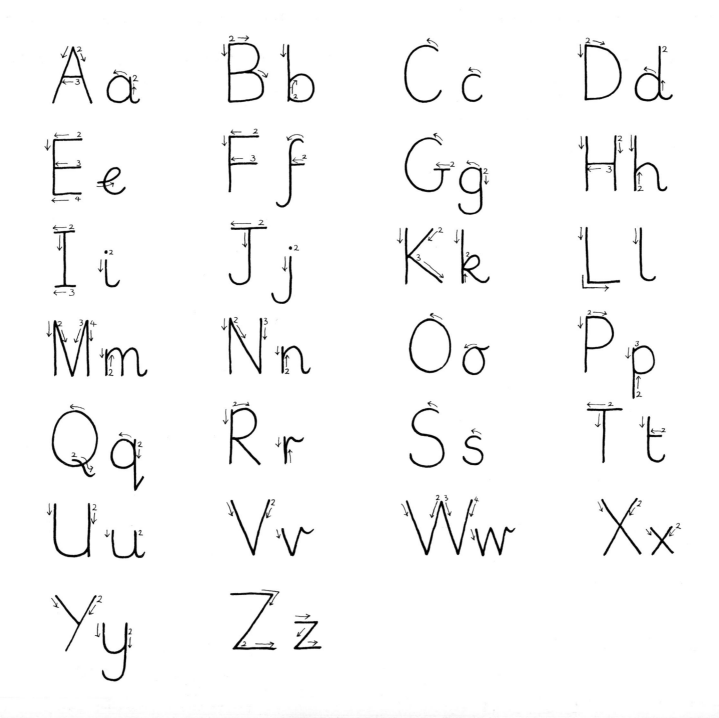

Name ....

Write the word I in each box to make words.

Cover each word and write it from memory.

☐ 'll   _____

☐ 've   _____

☐ 'm   _____

Now finish the puzzle.

I will = [I'll]

I am   = [   ]

I have = [   ]

Now use these words to finish the rhyme.

_____ painted green, red and blue,

_____ an upstairs and downstairs,

_____ take you to school.

What am I ? [   ]

Name ....

Write the word an in each box to make words.

Cover each word and write it from memory.

☐ imal   _____

w ☐ t   _____

☐ y   _____

m ☐ y   _____

pi ☐ o   _____

b ☐ ☐ a   _____

Now use these words to make your own word search.
Try it on a friend.

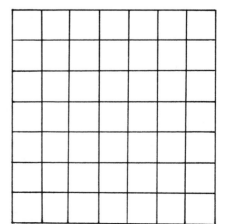

Write the word **as** in each box to make words.

Cover each word and write it from memory.

w☐ _____   w☐n't _____

h☐ _____   h☐n't _____

g☐ _____   ☐k _____

Now use **as** words to finish the sentences.

1. The boy _____ used the crossing.
2. The driver _____ driving carefully.
3. The policeman _____ed the boy what had happened.
What did the boy say?

Write the letter pattern **au** in each box to make words.

Cover each word and write it from memory.

s☐ce _____

s☐cer _____

☐tumn _____

l☐nch _____

c☐se _____

bec☐se _____

Now use some of these words to finish the phrases.

cup and _____

falling _____ leaves

_____ the rocket

tomato _____

© **LDA** A Hand for Spelling Activity Book 3

Name ....

Write the letter pattern *ew* in each box to make words.

Cover each word and write it from memory.

n [ ] _____

f [ ] _____

bl [ ] _____

fl [ ] _____

s [ ] _____

Write these words in alphabetical order

Now finish the pattern.

	newest
few	

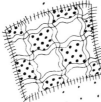

Now use the other words to finish the sentences.

1. _____ on a patch.

2. The plane _____ high.

3. The driver _____ his horn.

Name ....

Write the letter pattern *ey* in each box to make words.

Cover each word and write it from memory.

th [ ] _____

gr [ ] _____

ob [ ] _____

disob [ ] _____

chimn [ ] _____

Now write these words on the alphabet snake.

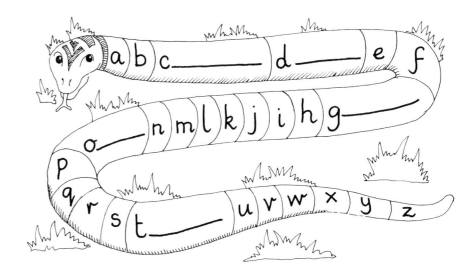

Write the letter pattern ie in each box to make words.

Cover each word and write it from memory.

l [ ]   _____

p [ ]   _____

t [ ]   _____

fr [ ] nd   _____

f [ ] ld   _____

qu [ ] t   _____

Write these words in alphabetical order

Now finish the pattern.

one	more than one add 's'
	lies
pie	
tie	
friend	
	fields

Write the word on in each box to make words.

Cover each word and write it from memory.

s [ ]   _____

[ ] ce   _____

[ ] ly   _____

cray [ ]   _____

ir [ ]   _____

Now sort out these jumbled sentences.

1. only They one had son.

_____

2. blue was The crayon broken.

_____

3. by Donald. won race The was

_____

4

Name ....

Write the letter pattern ut in each box to make words.

Cover each word and write it from memory.

b[ ]   _____

sh[ ]   _____

b[ ]ter   _____

p[ ]   _____

Now sort out these jumbled sentences.

1. was of the The shut. door house

_____

2. the on bread. Susan butter the put

_____

3. went home. stayed I John but school to

_____

Name ....

Write the letter pattern ack in each box to make words.

Cover each word and write it from memory.

s[ ]   _____

b[ ]   _____

bl[ ]   _____

tr[ ]   _____

qu[ ]   _____

Write these words in alphabetical order

Now use some of these words to finish the story.

On Sport's Day I won the _____ race, but I tripped in the egg and spoon and fell flat on my _____. I flew round the _____ in the relay, but missed the _____ tyre in the obstacle race.

Name ....

Write the word **act** in each box to make words.

Cover each word and write it from memory.

☐ or _____

☐ ion _____

pr ☐ ise _____

pr ☐ ice _____

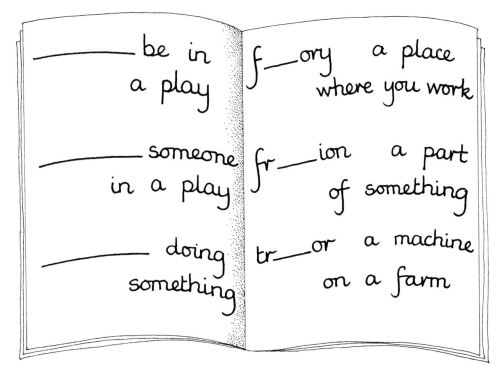
script

Now use **act** words to finish the dictionary list.

_____ be in a play

_____ someone in a play

_____ doing something

f__ory a place where you work

fr__ion a part of something

tr__or a machine on a farm

Name ....

Write the word **add** in each box to make words.

Cover each word and write it from memory.

☐ ress _____

☐ ition _____

l ☐ er _____

d ☐ y _____

p ☐ le _____

s ☐ le _____

Now write these words from memory on the ladder.

The opposite of subtraction is _____ .

Name ....

Write the letter pattern *ade* in each box to make words.

Cover each word and write it from memory.

m [ ] _____   sh [ ] _____

sp [ ] _____   bl [ ] _____

Now finish the crossword.

Across

1. A knife has one of these
4. A baby sits on its mother's _____
5. When it's sunny we sit in this

Down

1. The same as 1 across
2. A young boy
3. A kind of monkey
5. Used for digging

Name ....

Write the word *age* in each box to make words.

Cover each word and write it from memory.

c [ ] _____

r [ ] _____

st [ ] _____

band [ ] _____

cott [ ] _____

gar [ ] _____

Now use some of these words to write about the picture.
Remember to use capital letters and full stops.

_____

_____

_____

_____

Name ....

Write the word **aid** in each box to make words.

Cover each word and write it from memory.

m ☐ _____

r ☐ _____

l ☐ _____

p ☐ _____

afr ☐ _____

s ☐ _____

Write these words in alphabetical order

Now write these words from memory on the coconuts.

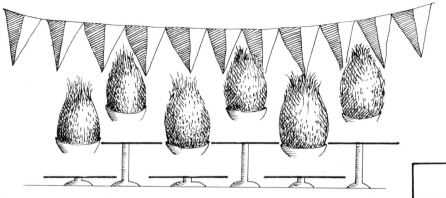

How many coconuts did you knock down? ☐

Name ....

Write the letter pattern **ail** in each box to make words.

Cover each word and write it from memory.

t ☐ _____   f ☐ _____

s ☐ _____   sn ☐ _____

n ☐ _____   tr ☐ _____

Now write these words from memory on the sails.

Now answer the questions.

1. The opposite of head is _____.

2. The opposite of pass is _____.

© LDA A Hand for Spelling Activity Book 3

Write the letter pattern *ain* in each box to make words.

Cover each word and write it from memory.

m⬜ _____

p⬜t _____

ch⬜ _____

pl⬜ _____

ag⬜ _____

ag⬜st _____

How many of these words can you find in the word search?

s	e	a	g	a	i	n	t	s
p	a	i	n	t	e	y	e	d
o	r	e	m	a	n	i	n	s
b	l	a	i	p	a	i	n	l
P	l	a	i	n	i	d	e	y
e	n	d	m	a	i	n	s	d
a	i	n	f	i	a	e	m	t
P	j	c	h	a	i	n	e	r
f	a	g	a	i	n	s	t	y

Write the word *air* in each box to make words.

Cover each word and write it from memory.

h⬜ _____

ch⬜ _____

p⬜ _____

f⬜ _____

d⬜y _____

⬜port _____

Now finish the patterns.

	hairs
chair	
	pairs
airport	

hair	
	fairy

Which word didn't you use? ⬜

Name ....

Write the letter pattern *ais* in each box to make words.

Cover each word and write it from memory.

r [ ] e _____

pr [ ] e _____

d [ ] y _____

d [ ] ies _____

Now finish the pattern.

raise		raising	
	praises		praised

Now use vowels [a e i o u] to finish these words.

r _ _ s _ _____   d _ _ sy _____

pr _ _ s _ _____   d _ _ s _ _ s _____

Name ....

Write the letter pattern *ake* in each box to make words.

Cover each word and write it from memory.

m [ ] _____

t [ ] _____

w [ ] _____

b [ ] _____

sn [ ] _____

sh [ ] _____

Write these words in alphabetical order

Now use *ake* words to finish the spell.

Catch four _____,

Add seven purple mice

And _____ them in a pan

_____ the magic sign

And _____ them when you can.

© LDA A Hand for Spelling Activity Book 3

Write the word *ale* in each box to make words.

Cover each word and write it from memory.

s[ ] _____   t[ ] _____

g[ ] _____   p[ ] _____

Imagine you are a sailor. Write your story in the speech marks using some of these words. Remember to use capital letters and full stops.

"

_____

_____

_____

"

_____

Write the word *all* in each box to make words.

Cover each word and write it from memory.

c[ ] _____

h[ ] _____

sm[ ] _____

sh[ ]ow _____

[ ]ow _____

v[ ]ey _____

Now print these words to fill the boxes.

Name ....

Write the word **amp** in each box to make words.

Cover each word and write it from memory.

c [ ] _____   l [ ] _____

d [ ] _____   st [ ] _____

Now read through this holiday postcard and correct the spelling and punctuation mistakes.

August 5th

Our campp site is by a small streem which fluded last nite. all our clothes got dampt and the lamp went out. Poor dad fell over Haveing a great time. Love Hary

ps Pleese save the stamp.

Name ....

Write the word **and** in each box to make words.

Cover each word and write it from memory.

h [ ] _____

l [ ] _____

s [ ] _____

s [ ] als _____

b [ ] age _____

isl [ ] _____

Change the h in hand to l, s, b, w

_____ _____ _____ _____

This funny saying may help you to remember **island**.

An island is land surrounded by water.

© LDA A Hand for Spelling Activity Book 3

Write the letter pattern **ang** in each box to make words.

Cover each word and write it from memory.

s[ ] _____   r[ ] _____

h[ ] _____   b[ ] _____

Now finish the patterns.

sing		
		rang
	springing	

	hangs	
		banging
clang		

Write the letter pattern **ank** in each box to make words.

Cover each word and write it from memory.

s[ ] _____

t[ ] _____

b[ ] _____

dr[ ] _____

bl[ ] _____

bl[ ]et _____

Now sort out these jumbled sentences.

1. tank   sank   The   mud.   the   in   large

_____

2. the   on   blankets   Those   go   bed.   double

_____

3. robbed   bank   night.   last   was   The

_____

Name ....

Write the word **ant** in each box to make words.

Cover each word and write it from memory.

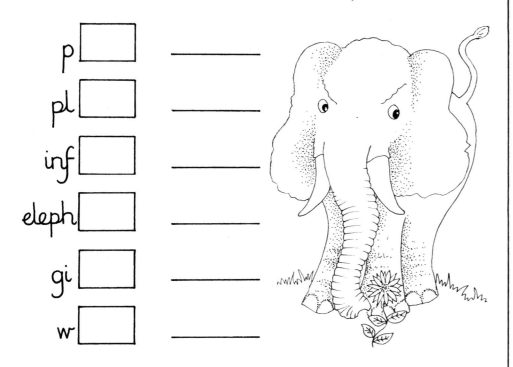

p [ ] _____

pl [ ] _____

inf [ ] _____

eleph [ ] _____

gi [ ] _____

w [ ] _____

Now use some of these words to finish the sentences.

1. A young child is an _____.

2. We _____ seeds in the garden.

3. An _____ is a large animal.

4. Humpty Dumpty was a _____ egg.

5. He _____ed to climb the tree.

Name ....

Write the word **any** in each box to make words.

Cover each word and write it from memory.

[ ]body _____   [ ]one _____

[ ]thing _____   [ ]how _____

[ ]way _____   [ ]where _____

Now use the words in the box to make new words.

one	how	body	where	way

any	no	some
_____	_____	_____
_____	_____	_____
_____	_____	_____
_____	_____	_____
_____	_____	_____

© LDA A Hand for Spelling Activity Book 3

Write the word *ape* in each box to make words.

Cover each word and write it from memory.

t ☐ _____

p ☐ r _____

gr ☐ s _____

esc ☐ _____

tr ☐ eze _____

Now finish the shopping list and answer the questions.

4 lb _____

5 rolls of _____

2 reels of _____

Which two couldn't you buy?

☐ ☐

Write the letter pattern *ard* in each box to make words.

Cover each word and write it from memory.

c ☐ _____

y ☐ _____

h ☐ _____

h ☐ ly _____

stand ☐ _____

Now print these words to fill the boxes.

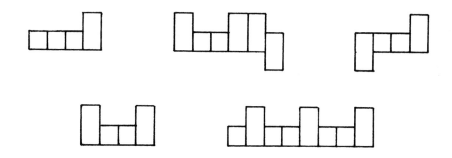

Name ....

Write the word *ark* in each box to make words.

Cover each word and write it from memory.

p[   ]   _____

d[   ]   _____

b[   ]   _____

m[   ]   _____

m[   ]et   _____

Now look at the different word endings we can make from

park. Now do the same with *mark* and *bark*.

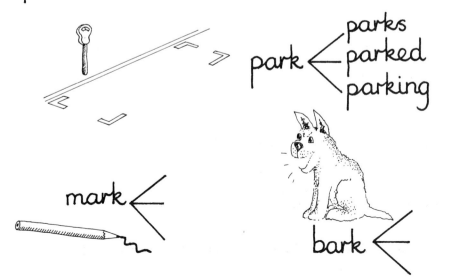

park ⟨ parks
       parked
       parking

mark ⟨

bark ⟨

16

Name ....

Write the word *arm* in each box to make words.

Cover each word and write it from memory.

[   ]y   _____

h[   ]   _____

f[   ]   _____

w[   ]   _____

Now write these words from memory on the farm carts.

Which word means the same as

fairly hot? [   ]

Name ....

Write the word *art* in each box to make words.

Cover each word and write it from memory.

sm[   ]   _____

[   ]icle   _____

qu[   ]er   _____

Now find all the *art* words.

partarticlewartquarterdartsmart

Name ....

Write the letter pattern *ary* in each box to make words.

Cover each word and write it from memory.

can[   ]   _____

secret[   ]   _____

libr[   ]   _____

diction[   ]   _____

necess[   ]   _____

Dictionary

Now use these words to finish the dictionary list.

_____ a yellow bird

_____ a book which tells you about words

_____ a place where books are kept

_____ needed very much

_____ works in an office

This funny saying may help you to remember _____ .

<u>n</u>ever <u>e</u>at <u>c</u>heese <u>e</u>at <u>s</u>ausage <u>s</u>andwiches <u>a</u>nd <u>r</u>emain <u>y</u>oung

Name ....

Write the letter pattern *ase* in each box to make words.

Cover each word and write it from memory.

b[ ] _____

c[ ] _____

ch[ ] _____

Now write these words from memory in your holiday suitcase.

Which word means the same as:

to run after? [   ]

a bag? [   ]

Name ....

Write the word *ash* in each box to make words.

Cover each word and write it from memory.

r[ ] _____   d[ ] _____

sm[ ] _____   cr[ ] _____

Now use some of these words to finish the sentence.

At the speedway racing cars

_____ , _____ and _____ .

Can you make these new *ash* words?

(l) (m) (g) → [ash]   _____ _____ _____

© **LDA** A Hand for Spelling Activity Book 3

Write the word *ass* in each box to make words.

Cover each word and write it from memory.

gr[ ]   _____

d[ ]   _____

d[ ]es   _____

[ ]embly   _____

Now use these words to finish the phrases.

tall, waving _____

morning _____

a _____ of children

two music _____

Can you make these new *ass* words?

br_____   p_____   l_____

_____   _____   _____

Write the letter pattern *ast* in each box to make words.

Cover each word and write it from memory.

p[ ]   _____

l[ ]   _____

f[ ]   _____

m[ ]er   _____

c[ ]le   _____

breakf[ ]   _____

Write these words in alphabetical order

Write the beginning of the story in the picture.
Remember to use capital letters and full stops.

_____

_____

_____

_____

_____

Name ....

Write the word *ate* in each box to make words.

Cover each word and write it from memory.

m ☐ _____

l ☐ _____

g ☐ _____

d ☐ _____

pl ☐ _____

w ☐ r _____

Now finish the pattern.

mate	
	gates
	dates
plate	

Change the l in late to d, h, sl, cr

_____ _____ _____ _____

Name ....

Write the letter pattern *ath* in each box to make words.

Cover each word and write it from memory.

b ☐ _____

f ☐ er _____

p ☐ _____

g ☐ er _____

b ☐ e _____

Now sort out these jumbled sentences.

1. he rather the father My sea. would bathe in said

_____

_____

2. gather along path. We blackberries the will this

_____

Name ....

Write the letter pattern *ave* in each box to make words.

Cover each word and write it from memory.

w[ ] _____   br[ ] _____

g[ ] _____   h[ ] _____

c[ ] _____   tr[ ]l _____

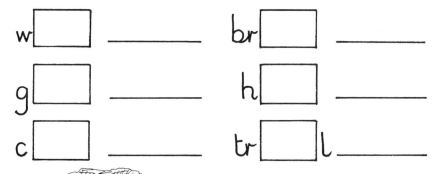

Now use these words to finish the puzzles.

This is often dark and gloomy. [ ]

This word moves about. [ ]

This word is on water. [ ]

If you save someone you are [ ]

If you passed a book you [ ] it

If something is yours you [ ] it

Name ....

Write the letter pattern *awn* in each box to make words.

Cover each word and write it from memory.

l[ ] _____

d[ ] _____

y[ ] _____

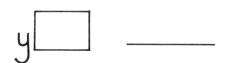

Now add an *s* to these words to make plurals.

lawn + s _____

dawn + s _____

yawn + s _____

Now find the small words in the following words.

lawnmower	yawning	drawn

Name ....

Write the letter pattern **bur** in each box to make words.

Cover each word and write it from memory.

☐n _____

☐nt _____

☐y _____

☐ied _____

Now finish the patterns.

	+ s	+ ing	+ ed	+ t
burn				
turn				/////

	burying		
worry			
		hurries	
			married

Name ....

Write the word **bus** in each box to make words.

Cover each word and write it from memory.

☐y _____

☐iness _____

☐h _____

Now write these words from memory on the bus.

This funny saying may help you to remember **business.**

The <u>busy</u> man went to <u>business</u>

on a <u>bus</u>.

© LDA A Hand for Spelling Activity Book 3

Write the word *can* in each box to make words.

Cover each word and write it from memory.

☐ e _____

☐ dle _____

☐ not _____

☐ 't _____

☐ oe _____

☐ ary _____

Now write these words from memory in the river.

_____   _____   _____

_____   _____   _____

Which word means can't?   ☐

Which word means a narrow boat?   ☐

Write the word *cap* in each box to make words.

Cover each word and write it from memory.

☐ ture _____

☐ ital _____

☐ tain _____

Imagine you are the captain of a ship. Write your story in the speech marks using some of these words. Remember to use capital letters and full stops.

"
_____
_____
_____
_____
                                        "
                                         .

Write the letter pattern *cei* in each box to make words.

Cover each word and write it from memory.

[ ] ling _____

re [ ] ve _____

re [ ] pt _____

Now use these words to finish the puzzles.

Write the word which means you are given something. [ ]

Write the word which describes part of a room. [ ]

You are given this when you pay a bill. [ ]

Write the letter pattern *cou* in each box to make words.

Cover each word and write it from memory.

[ ] sin _____

[ ] ple _____

[ ] ntry _____

[ ] ld _____

[ ] nter _____

[ ] rt _____

Now write these words from memory on the shop counter.

Which word means two? [ ]

Which word is a relation? [ ]

Name ....

Write the word **day** in each box to make words.

Cover each word and write it from memory.

Mon [ ] _____   Fri [ ] _____

Tues [ ] _____   Satur [ ] _____

Wednes [ ] _____   Sun [ ] _____

Thurs [ ] _____

Now write the day of the week for each activity.

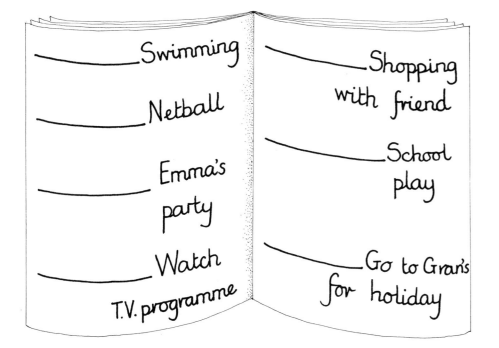

_____ Swimming

_____ Netball

_____ Emma's party

_____ Watch T.V. programme

_____ Shopping with friend

_____ School play

_____ Go to Gran's for holiday

Name ....

Write the word **die** in each box to make words.

Cover each word and write it from memory.

[ ] s _____

bo [ ] s _____

la [ ] s _____

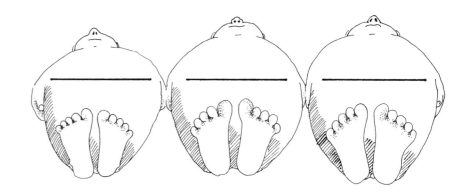

Now write these words from memory on the bodies.

Now write out this sentence.

We all try to eat a healthy diet.

_____

© LDA A Hand for Spelling Activity Book 3

Write the letter pattern *ead* in each box to make words.

Cover each word and write it from memory.

d[ ] _____

inst[ ] _____

b[ ] _____

r[ ] _____

l[ ] _____

l[ ]er _____

Now match the following words with a picture.

leader

read

bread

spread

Write the letter pattern *eak* in each box to make words.

Cover each word and write it from memory.

sp[ ] _____

st[ ] _____

br[ ] _____

br[ ]fast _____

Now use *eak* words to finish the puzzles.

A kind of meat

In the middle of the morning

The first meal of the day

You move your lips to do this

The top of a mountain

Water dripping from a tap

[ ]

[ ]

[ ]

[ ]

[ ]

[ ]

Name ....

Write the letter pattern *eal* in each box to make words.

Cover each word and write it from memory.

m [ ]   _____

s [ ]   _____

d [ ]   _____

r [ ]ly   _____

h [ ]th   _____

h [ ]thy _____

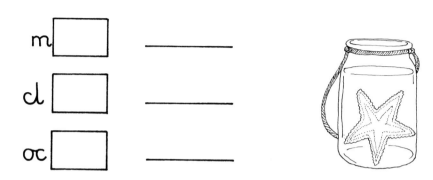

Now finish the story using some of these words.
Remember to use capital letters and full stops.

On the shore by the sea, a

large seal ate a _____

_____

_____

Name ....

Write the letter pattern *ean* in each box to make words.

Cover each word and write it from memory.

m [ ]   _____

cl [ ]   _____

oc [ ]   _____

Now use some of these words to write a seaside poster.

Come to Lean-on-Sea for your
holiday

© LDA A Hand for Spelling Activity Book 3

Write the word *ear* in each box to make words.

Cover each word and write it from memory.

n ☐ _____

t ☐ _____

w ☐ _____

☐ n _____

l ☐ n _____

☐ ly _____

Now finish the pattern.

tear		
	wears	
		earning
learn		
	hears	

Write the letter pattern *eas* in each box to make words.

Cover each word and write it from memory.

☐ y _____

☐ ily _____

r ☐ on _____

s ☐ on _____

tr ☐ ure _____

pl ☐ ure _____

treasure map

Now write a story about digging for the treasure using some of these words. Remember to use capital letters and full stops.

The reason we found _____

_____

_____

_____

© LDA A Hand for Spelling Activity Book 3

Write the word *eat* in each box to make words.

Cover each word and write it from memory.

n ☐ _____

s ☐ _____

m ☐ _____

gr ☐ _____

th ☐ re _____

l ☐ her _____

How many of these words can you find in the word search?

l	n	e	a	t	e	d	t	m
b	a	e	t	m	e	e	l	s
e	g	r	e	a	t	d	r	e
t	h	e	a	t	r	e	d	s
a	e	l	e	a	t	h	e	r
b	a	t	h	j	k	e	a	m
e	s	e	a	t	t	u	v	a
d	e	f	m	e	a	t	e	a

Write the letter pattern *ect* in each box to make words.

Cover each word and write it from memory.

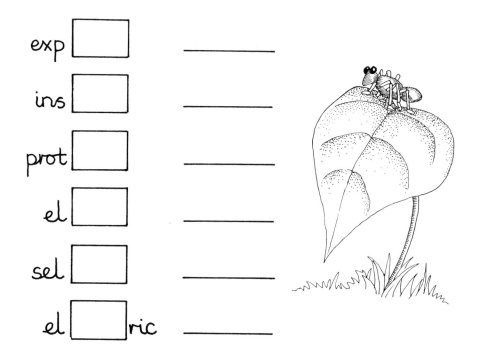

exp ☐ _____

ins ☐ _____

prot ☐ _____

el ☐ _____

sel ☐ _____

el ☐ ric _____

Now print these words to fill the boxes.

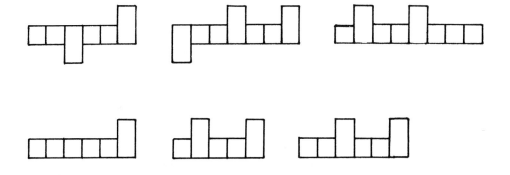

Name ....

Write the letter pattern *eed* in each box to make words.

Cover each word and write it from memory.

s[ ]   _____

f[ ]   _____

f[ ]ing _____

n[ ]   _____

n[ ]le   _____

Now use some of these words to finish the story.

Some birds like _____ and all birds _____ water for _____ and cleaning their feathers.

Name ....

Write the word *eel* in each box to make words.

Cover each word and write it from memory.

f[ ]   _____

st[ ]   _____

wh[ ]   _____

Now use *eel* words to finish the phrases.

orange _____

iron and _____

steering _____

wriggling _____

Change the f in feel to h, kn, st

_____ _____ _____

© LDA A Hand for Spelling Activity Book 3

Name ....

Write the letter pattern *een* in each box to make words.

Cover each word and write it from memory.

s☐ _____   betw☐ _____

b☐ _____

gr☐ _____

qu☐ _____

Now use these words to finish the rhyme.

Pussy cat, pussy cat,

Where have you _____?

I've _____ up to London

And I've _____ the _____.

She sat on a throne

Of gold, red and _____

Two guards at her side

The _____ in _____.

Name ....

Write the letter pattern *eer* in each box to make words.

Cover each word and write it from memory.

ch☐ _____

ch☐ful _____

d☐ _____

qu☐ _____

Now sort out these jumbled sentences.

1. cheer from football A came the ground.

_____

2. deer The the wood. in were

_____

3. clown face. cheerful a The had

_____

Name ....

Write the letter pattern *eet* in each box to make words.

Cover each word and write it from memory.

m[ ] _____

f[ ] _____

sh[ ] _____

sw[ ] _____

str[ ] _____

t[ ]h _____

Now finish the pattern.

sheet	
	streets
sweet	

Now write the plurals of these words.

foot [   ]   tooth [   ]

Name ....

Write the letter pattern *ell* in each box to make words.

Cover each word and write it from memory.

sm[ ] _____   sh[ ] _____

sw[ ] _____   j[ ]y _____

sp[ ] _____   y[ ]ow _____

Now use these words to finish the puzzles.

A bright colour   [   ]

The thin part of an egg   [   ]

To get bigger   [   ]

To use the nose to sniff [   ]

To write a word correctly [   ]

A wobbly pudding   [   ]

© LDA A Hand for Spelling Activity Book 3

Write the letter pattern **elt** in each box to make words.

Cover each word and write it from memory.

m ☐ _____

b ☐ _____

f ☐ _____

Now use these words to finish the sentences.

1. Toys can be made of _____ cloth.

2. Ice-cream and snow _____ in the sun.

3. Trousers and skirts have a _____.

Now finish the pattern.

feel	
	knelt

Write the word **end** in each box to make words.

Cover each word and write it from memory.

s ☐ _____

l ☐ _____

b ☐ _____

sp ☐ _____

fri ☐ _____

Write these words in alphabetical order

Now finish the pattern.

send			
	lends		
		bending	
			spent

Name ....

Write the letter pattern *ent* in each box to make words.

Cover each word and write it from memory.

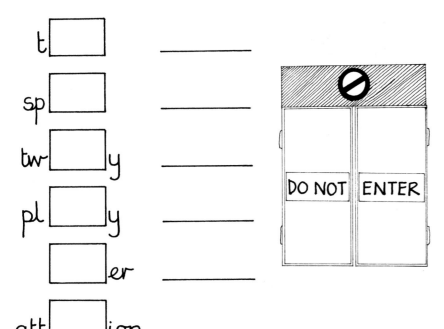

t☐ _____

sp☐ _____

tw☐y _____

pl☐y _____

☐er _____

att☐ion _____

DO NOT | ENTER

Now sort out these jumbled sentences.

1. rain through tent. The leaked the

_____

2. friends Twenty to party. the came

_____

3. spent games. playing the They time

Name ....

Write the letter pattern *err* in each box to make words.

Cover each word and write it from memory.

m☐y _____

b☐y _____

ch☐y _____

t☐ible _____

How many *err* words can you find in the word search?

e	r	m	e	r	r	y	s	b	e
t	e	r	r	o	r	a	r	e	s
e	r	r	c	h	e	r	r	y	e
i	t	e	r	r	i	b	l	e	d
e	b	e	r	r	y	e	r	r	y
s	e	b	e	r	r	o	r	d	s

© LDA A Hand for Spelling Activity Book 3

Write the letter pattern *est* in each box to make words.

Cover each word and write it from memory.

t☐ _____

ch☐ _____

qu☐ion _____

cont☐ _____

w☐ern _____

orch☐ra _____

Now write these words from memory.

_____ _____ _____

_____ _____

Now answer the questions.

1. The opposite of answer is _____ .

2. The opposite of eastern is _____ .

Name ....

Write the letter pattern *ett* in each box to make words.

Cover each word and write it from memory.

l☐er _____

b☐er _____

l☐uce _____

s☐le _____

s☐ing _____

pr☐y _____

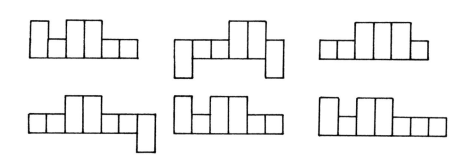

Now print these words to fill the boxes.

Name ....

Write the letter pattern *exc* in each box to make words.

Cover each word and write it from memory.

☐	ept	_____
☐	use	_____
☐	iting	_____
☐	itement	_____

Now use these words to finish the sentences.

1. She won a very _____ race.

2. Everyone had a prize _____ me.

3. There was a lot of _____ when Paul won the match.

4. Her _____ for being late was that she had missed the bus.

Name ....

Write the letter pattern *fam* in each box to make words.

Cover each word and write it from memory.

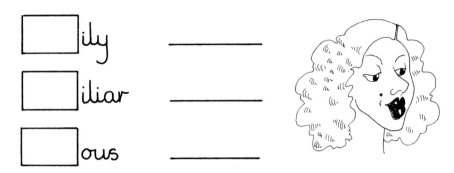

☐	ily	_____
☐	iliar	_____
☐	ous	_____

Now write these words from memory on the coach.

The opposite of _____ is unfamiliar.

© **LDA** A Hand for Spelling Activity Book 3

Name ....

Write the word *for* in each box to make words.

Cover each word and write it from memory.

☐ get   _____

☐ got   _____

☐ gotten _____

☐ est   _____

Now find the small words in the following words.

forest	forgotten	formation

The opposite of remember is _____.

Name ....

Write the letter pattern *ful* in each box to make words.

Cover each word and write it from memory.

aw ☐   _____

cheer ☐   _____

care ☐   _____

thank ☐   _____

wonder ☐   _____

beauti ☐   _____

Now add *ly* to make new words.

awful   awfully

beautiful   _____

careful   _____

wonderful   _____

cheerful   _____

Name ....

Write the letter pattern *gar* in each box to make words.

Cover each word and write it from memory.

[ ] den _____

[ ] age _____

su [ ] _____

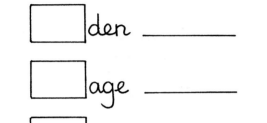

Now sort out these jumbled sentences.

1. do sugar tea. my in I have not

_____

2. flowers garden. the There many in were

_____

3. the Our car in garage. was new

_____

Name ....

Write the word *ice* in each box to make words.

Cover each word and write it from memory.

tw [ ] _____

off [ ] _____

pol [ ] man _____

pract [ ] _____

just [ ] _____

ju [ ] _____

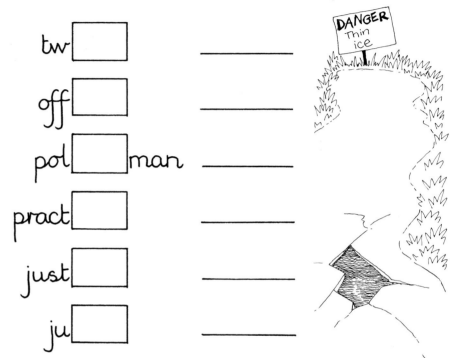

Now find the small words in the following words.

practice	policeman	notice

© LDA A Hand for Spelling Activity Book 3

Write the letter pattern _ick_ in each box to make words.

Cover each word and write it from memory.

p ☐ _____

k ☐ _____

br ☐ _____

tr ☐ _____

st ☐ _____

qu ☐ _____

Write these words in alphabetical order

Now finish the patterns.

pick		
	kicks	
		sticking

	sticky
trick	

Write the letter pattern _ide_ in each box to make words.

Cover each word and write it from memory.

h ☐ _____   sl ☐ _____

w ☐ _____   dec ☐ _____

r ☐ _____   ☐ a _____

Now read through this story and correct the spelling mistakes.

Mum had the idear of going to the funfair for the day. I coudn't wait to try out the slide. It was verey steep and we shouted with excitment. Mum tried it too, and then after tea we desided it was time to go home.

Name ....

Write the letter pattern *ife* in each box to make words.

Cover each word and write it from memory.

l [ ] _____

w [ ] _____

kn [ ] _____

Now finish the pattern.

one wife	
	two lives
one knife	

Now finish the phrases.

husband and _____

_____ and fork

Name ....

Write the letter pattern *ift* in each box to make words.

Cover each word and write it from memory.

l [ ] _____

g [ ] _____

dr [ ] _____

Now use these words to finish the story.

Every _____ in the store was full of people shopping. I was busy looking for a _____ for my friend. It took me ages to find the _____ I wanted.

On the bus going home I watched the snow _____ against the darkness of the sky.

Write the letter pattern *ine* in each box to make words.

Cover each word and write it from memory.

m ☐ _____

sh ☐ _____

mach ☐ _____

eng ☐ _____

imag ☐ _____

l ☐ n _____

Now write these words from memory on the engine.

The opposite of yours is _____ .

Write the letter pattern *ion* in each box to make words.

Cover each word and write it from memory.

l ☐ _____   un ☐ _____

mill ☐ _____   divis ☐ _____

reg ☐ _____

Now finish the story using some of these words. Remember to use capital letters and full stops.

In the long long ago, when the earth was young, a million lions lived on the great plains in Africa. They lay under the trees shading their bodies from the fierce sun. Then at night they hunted.

_____

_____

_____

Name ....

Write the letter pattern **irt** in each box to make words.

Cover each word and write it from memory.

d[ ] _____

d[ ]y _____

sh[ ] _____

th[ ]y _____

b[ ]h _____

b[ ]hday _____

Now use some of these words to finish the dictionary list.

1. _____ the day we remember when someone is born

2. _____ dust or mud

3. _____ clothing with sleeves

4. _____ a number

Name ....

Write the letter pattern **ist** in each box to make words.

Cover each word and write it from memory.

l[ ] _____

s[ ]er _____

m[ ]er _____

h[ ]ory _____

Chr[ ] _____

Chr[ ]mas _____

Now find the small words in the following words.

history	Christmas	whistle

Name ....

Write the letter pattern _ite_ in each box to make words.

Cover each word and write it from memory.

b[ ] _____

qu[ ] _____

inv[ ] _____

exc[ ]d _____

wr[ ]r _____

typewr[ ]r _____

Now finish the pattern.

Write these words in alphabetical order

bite		
	invites	
		exciting
write		

Name ....

Write the letter pattern _ive_ in each box to make words.

Cover each word and write it from memory.

d[ ] _____

dr[ ] _____

w[ ]s _____

kn[ ]s _____

arr[ ] _____

r[ ]r _____

Now finish the pattern.

Write these words in alphabetical order

dive		
	drives	
		arriving
give		
	lives	

Name ....

Write the word low in each box to make words.

Cover each word and write it from memory.

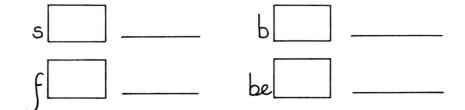

s [ ] _____   b [ ] _____

f [ ] _____   be [ ] _____

Now write these words from memory on the trumpet.

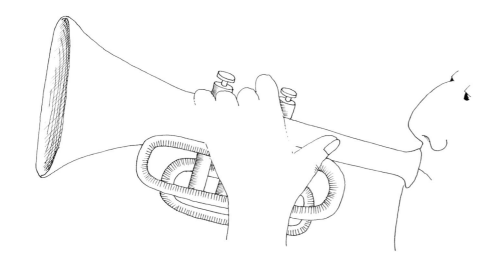

Now answer the questions.

1. The opposite of fast is _____ .

2. The opposite of above is _____ .

44

Name ....

Write the letter pattern oal in each box to make words.

Cover each word and write it from memory.

c [ ] _____

g [ ] _____

f [ ] _____

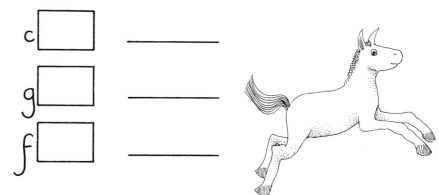

Now answer the questions.

1. Is the foal jumping?   Yes/No

2. Is this a goal?   Yes/No

3. Is the coal burning?   Yes/No

Name ....

Write the word *oat* in each box to make words.

Cover each word and write it from memory.

b[ ] _____   c[ ] _____

g[ ] _____   thr[ ] _____

Now use some of these words to finish the rhyme.

A large mountain _____
With a rough hairy _____
Came down from the hillside
one day.
He saw a big river
Stepped into a _____
With a yell and a shout
Sailed away.

Name ....

Write the letter pattern *ock* in each box to make words.

Cover each word and write it from memory.

l[ ] _____

r[ ] _____

p[ ]et _____

s[ ]s _____

d[ ] _____

st[ ] _____

Write these words in alphabetical order

Now write these words from memory on the rocks.

Which word is used for telling the time? [   ]

Name ....

Write the letter pattern **oes** in each box to make words.

Cover each word and write it from memory.

d[ ]oes _____   t[ ]oes _____

d[ ]n't _____   potat[ ]oes _____

g[ ]oes _____   sh[ ]oes _____

Now sort out these jumbled sentences.

1. doesn't potatoes. James like

_____

2. find her Susan not shoes. new could

_____

3. goes The bus London. to next

_____

Name ....

Write the letter pattern **oke** in each box to make words.

Cover each word and write it from memory.

w[ ] _____

aw[ ] _____

sm[ ] _____

br[ ] _____

Write these words in alphabetical order

Now finish the story using some of these words.
Remember to use capital letters and full stops.

On bonfire night we had a blazing fire. The fireworks flared into the sky. In the middle of the night Mum woke with a start _____

_____

_____

_____

© LDA A Hand for Spelling Activity Book 3

Name ....

Write the word **old** in each box to make words.

Cover each word and write it from memory.

c[ ] _____   h[ ] _____

f[ ] _____   s[ ] _____

t[ ] _____   s[ ]ier _____

Now sort out these jumbled sentences.

1. days November sometimes are cold. very

_____

2. soldiers told camp. The the were guard to

_____

3. you hold book me. please this for Would

_____

Name ....

Write the letter pattern **ome** in each box to make words.

Cover each word and write it from memory.

h[ ] _____

c[ ] _____

s[ ] _____

w[ ]n _____

Now use these words to finish the sentences.

1. The children were on their way _____.

2. I would like to _____ home with you.

3. There were ten _____ at the bus stop.

4. John wanted _____ more pudding.

Name ....

Write the word **one** in each box to make words.

Cover each word and write it from memory.

n[ ] _____   m[ ]y _____

g[ ] _____   h[ ]y _____

b[ ] _____

teleph[ ] _____

Now use some of these words to finish the poem.

Bears and bees

Both like _____ .

They'll pay any _____

For a really large pot,

And eat up the lot.

They're sad when it's _____

And there's _____ for tea.

48

Name ....

Write the letter pattern **ood** in each box to make words.

Cover each word and write it from memory.

g[ ] _____   w[ ] _____

st[ ] _____   f[ ] _____

fl[ ] _____   bl[ ] _____

Now read through this story and correct the spelling mistakes.

The woulden hut where we camped this yeer stood by the stream. We didn't think it would rian so heavily on our last nite, but soon there wos a flood. In the morning the hut and all our food had gon. But our friends in the next tent made a barbecue and soon we were haveing sausages and a really good meal.

Name ....

Write the letter pattern **ook** in each box to make words.

Cover each word and write it from memory.

c[ ] _____   h[ ] _____

t[ ] _____   l[ ] _____

b[ ] _____   sh[ ] _____

Now finish the patterns.

shake	shaken	
		took

cook			
	hooks		
		looking	
			booked

Name ....

Write the letter pattern **ool** in each box to make words.

Cover each word and write it from memory.

c[ ] _____

p[ ] _____

st[ ] _____

t[ ]s _____

sch[ ] _____

w[ ] _____

Write these words in alphabetical order

[ ]

How many **ool** words can you find in the word search?

h	y	p	e	c	o	o	l	i
f	l	k	s	c	h	o	o	l
e	p	o	o	l	s	e	d	y
r	e	t	o	o	l	s	e	t
o	v	w	o	o	l	l	e	n
f	o	o	l	b	r	o	o	s
e	m	n	d	s	t	o	o	l
e	w	o	o	l	e	r	s	o
o	o	f	o	o	l	i	s	h

[ ]

Write the letter pattern *oom* in each box to make words.

Cover each word and write it from memory.

r [ ] _____

bedr [ ] _____

bl [ ] _____

gl [ ] y _____

Now use the apostrophe.

the room of

Gran's room

_____

the car of

Mum's car

_____

the room of

David's bedroom

_____

the cake of

Maria's cake

_____

Write the letter pattern *oon* in each box to make words.

Cover each word and write it from memory.

s [ ] _____

m [ ] _____

n [ ] _____

sp [ ] _____

Write these words in alphabetical order

Now use these words to finish the sentences.

1. There will be a full _____ tonight.

2. And the dish ran away with the _____.

3. Dad will be home very _____.

4. Betty liked her lunch at _____.

Name ....

Write the letter pattern oot in each box to make words.

Cover each word and write it from memory.

r ☐ _____   sh ☐ _____

b ☐ _____   f ☐ _____

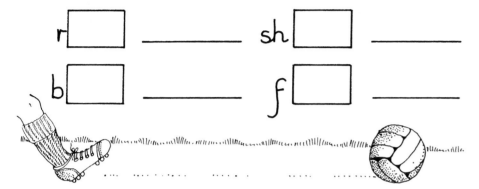

Now read through this story and correct the spelling mistakes.

All the year I'd wonted to play
in the school team but either
somone else was chosen, or we
were away on an outing.
At last my chance came. I dreamt
of the moment when the ball
would shute of my foot and
I'd score the winning goal.

Name ....

Write the letter pattern orn in each box to make words.

Cover each word and write it from memory.

h ☐ _____   c ☐ er _____

b ☐ _____   w ☐ _____

c ☐ _____   m ☐ ing _____

Now use some of these words to finish the puzzles.

The early part of the day ☐

Used to sound a warning
from a car ☐

Breakfast flakes are made
of this ☐

A birthday celebrates the day
we were .... ☐

A square room has four
of these .... ☐

Name ....

Write the letter pattern **ost** in each box to make words.

Cover each word and write it from memory.

c▢ _____   m▢ _____

fr▢ _____   alm▢ _____

p▢ _____   gh▢ _____

Now finish the story using some of these words.
Remember to use capital letters and full stops.

I woke early on my birthday. I
couldn't wait for the postman
to bring my cards. It was almost
time for school when I saw a
strange shape _____

_____

_____

52

Name ....

Write the letter pattern **oth** in each box to make words.

Cover each word and write it from memory.

cl▢ _____

b▢er _____

b▢ _____

cl▢es _____

cl▢ing _____

Now write these words from memory on the clothes line.

Now answer the questions.

1. The same as two is _____ .

2. The same as annoy is _____ .

Write the letter pattern **ott** in each box to make words.

Cover each word and write it from memory.

b [ ] om _____

c [ ] on _____

b [ ] le _____

thr [ ] le _____

c [ ] age _____

Now use these words to finish the dictionary list.

_____ it holds lemonade

_____ the lowest part

_____ a small house

_____ thread for sewing

_____ part of an engine

Write the letter pattern **oud** in each box to make words.

Cover each word and write it from memory.

l [ ] _____   al [ ] _____

d [ ] _____   pr [ ] _____

Now finish the pattern.

	louder	
proud		proudest

Now write out this sentence.

The aeroplane disappeared into the clouds.

_____

_____

Name ....

Write the word *our* in each box to make words.

Cover each word and write it from memory.

h[ ] _____   fav[ ]ite _____

fl[ ] _____   j[ ]ney _____

p[ ] _____

col[ ] _____

hon[ ] _____

neighb[ ] _____

Now finish the pattern.

hour	
	colours
	neighbours
favourite	

Name ....

Write the word *out* in each box to make words.

Cover each word and write it from memory.

ab[ ] _____

sh[ ] _____

tr[ ] _____

r[ ]e _____

Now use *out* words to finish the poem.

When we're _____ and _____

We sing and we _____

We make such a din and a fuss.

If we can't read the map,

Or follow the _____

We get out and hop on a bus.

© LDA A Hand for Spelling Activity Book 3

Write the letter pattern *ove* in each box to make words.

Cover each word and write it from memory.

m ☐ ____   pr ☐ ____

dr ☐ ____   st ☐ ____

ab ☐ ____   gl ☐ ____

Now finish the pattern.

move		
	proved	
		loving
shove		

Now use *ove* words to finish the sentence.

Put the c___r ___r the chair.

_____

Write the word *own* in each box to make words.

Cover each word and write it from memory.

t ☐ ____

d ☐ ____

cl ☐ ____

kn ☐ ____

Now read through this story and correct the spelling mistakes.

If he had knowen the buket was full of water the cloun would have run away. But he was soaked. He sliped and slithered as he ran accross the ring, until finally he fell over.

Name ....

Write the letter pattern *par* in each box to make words.

Cover each word and write it from memory.

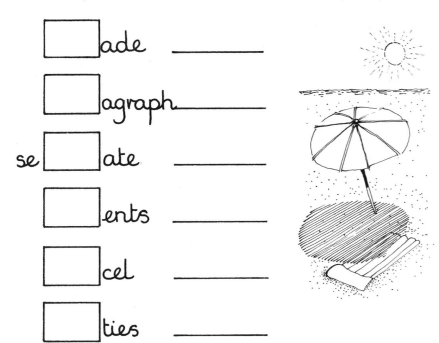

☐ade _____

☐agraph _____

se☐ate _____

☐ents _____

☐cel _____

☐ties _____

Now write these words from memory on the parachutes.

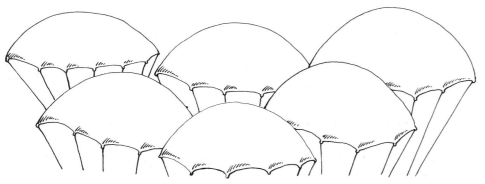

The same as package is _____.

Name ....

Write the word *pen* in each box to make words.

Cover each word and write it from memory.

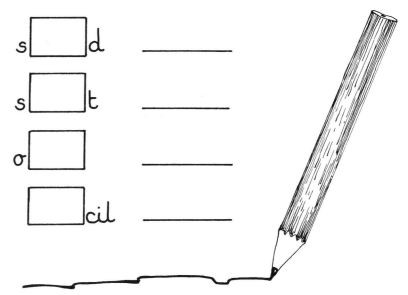

s☐d _____

s☐t _____

o☐ _____

☐cil _____

Now use these words to spend your holiday money.

I had £2 for my birthday.
I _____ 50p on a pen and _____.
I will _____ 50p on a puzzle book. How much money did I have left to _____ a new bank account? ☐

© LDA A Hand for Spelling Activity Book 3

Write the letter pattern *per* in each box to make words.

Cover each word and write it from memory.

[ ] haps _____

[ ] son _____

[ ] fume _____

[ ] iod _____

Now use these words to finish the dictionary list.

_____ a pleasant smell

_____ possibly something may happen

_____ a length of time

_____ a man, woman or child

Write the letter pattern *pro* in each box to make words.

Cover each word and write it from memory.

[ ] mise _____

[ ] bably _____

[ ] gramme _____

Now sort out these jumbled sentences.

1. probably swimming I go lunch. after will

_____

2. friend. gave promise my I my to

_____

3. favourite programme. my TV missed I

_____

4. you the Can program computer?

_____

Write the word **raw** in each box to make words.

Cover each word and write it from memory.

st[ ]raw   _____

d[ ]raw   _____

d[ ]er   _____

Now write a sentence about each picture.

_____

_____

_____

Write the word **ree** in each box to make words.

Cover each word and write it from memory.

t[ ]ree   _____

th[ ]ree   _____

refe[ ]ree   _____

Now answer the questions.

1. Is this eret losing its leaves?   Yes/No

What was the word?   _____

2. Does the football fereere have a   Yes/No

whistle? What was the word?   _____

3. Does four come before reeht?   Yes/No

What was the word?   _____

Write the letter pattern rew in each box to make words.

Cover each word and write it from memory.

d[ ] _____

g[ ] _____

th[ ] _____

Now finish the pattern.

	I will	I have
grew	grow	
drew		drawn
threw		

The opposite of caught is _____ .

Write the word row in each box to make words.

Cover each word and write it from memory.

g[ ] _____

th[ ] _____

ar[ ] _____

nar[ ] _____

Now read through this story and correct the spelling mistakes.

From inside the castel they saw the army throgh the trees. They had a large pile of stones redy to throw, and arrows to fire through the narow windows. When they saw so meny soldiers they were afrade. One man escaped in a small boat which he rowd across the moat.

Write the word **see** in each box to make words.

Cover each word and write it from memory.

☐ d_____		☐ k _____
☐ m_____		☐ -saw_____

Now use **see** words to finish the sentences.

1. The teacher did not _____ very well.

2. The dog was last _____ near the park.

3. The plant had grown from a tiny _____ .

4. The children played on the _____ and then played hide-and-_____ .

Write the word **the** in each box to make words.

Cover each word and write it from memory.

☐ m _____		☐ n _____
☐ se _____		☐ re _____
☐ ir _____		☐ y _____

Now use the letters in the tree to make words starting with **the** .

Now write out this sentence.

Their books are over there.

_____

Name ....

Write the letter pattern **tor** in each box to make words.

Cover each word and write it from memory.

☐ n _____

s ☐ y _____

his ☐ y _____

trac ☐ _____

visi ☐ _____

Write these words in alphabetical order

Now use some of these words to finish the story.

The _____ told us the _____ about life in her country. In the villages the people worked on the land. It was hard. Then a _____ was sent and they were able to grow more food.

Name ....

Write the letter pattern **tru** in each box to make words.

Cover each word and write it from memory.

☐ nk _____

☐ ck _____

☐ st _____

☐ e _____

☐ th _____

☐ ly _____

my trunks

Now write these words from memory on the side of the truck.

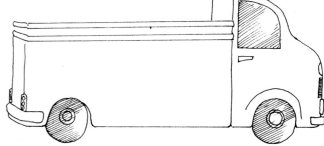

Now finish the sentence.

Peter said he was telling the _____.

Write the letter pattern **uck** in each box to make words.

Cover each word and write it from memory.

l☐ _____   b☐et _____

d☐ _____

Now use **uck** words to finish the story.

In the wood lived an old man, his wife, and their pet _____. The old man was unlucky. His hens didn't lay eggs and his corn didn't grow. Then one day his _____ came into the house carrying a _____ in its beak. And what do you think was in the bucket?

_____

_____

And that was the start of his good _____.

Write the letter pattern **udd** in each box to make words.

Cover each word and write it from memory.

m☐y _____

s☐en _____

m☐le _____

p☐le _____

p☐ing _____

Now use these words to finish the phrases.

quick is _____

hot sponge and jam is a _____

soil and water are _____

a mess is a _____

a pool of water is a _____

© LDA A Hand for Spelling Activity Book 3

Name ....

Write the letter pattern *uit* in each box to make words.

Cover each word and write it from memory.

bisc 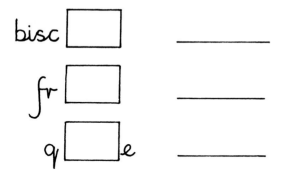 _____

fr _____

q e _____

Now write these words from memory on your tracksuit.

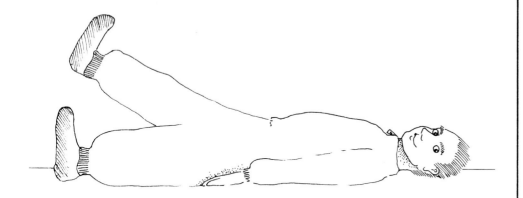

Now write out this sentence.

The biscuit was quite fruity.

_____

Name ....

Write the letter pattern *ull* in each box to make words.

Cover each word and write it from memory.

b _____

f _____

p _____

Now use *ull* words to finish the crossword.

Across

3. A large farm animal
5. To drag something to you
6. Not cheerful

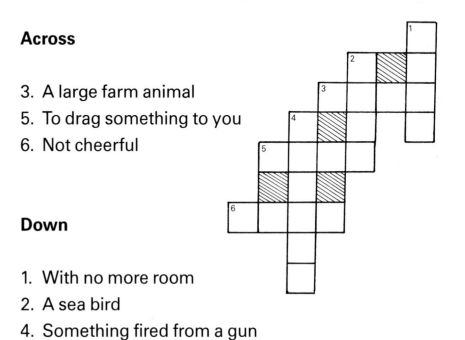

Down

1. With no more room
2. A sea bird
4. Something fired from a gun

Name ....

Write the letter pattern umb in each box to make words.

Cover each word and write it from memory.

d [ ] _____

th [ ] _____

n [ ] er _____

3
1 7 4
2 8
5 9
6
1 0

The shaded letters are called vowels.
The others are called consonants.

| a b c d e f g h i j k l m n o p q r s t u v w x y z |

Now find the vowel to finish the puzzle.

6 1
8
7 5
1
4 5
8 9 0
3

n_mb_rs [   ]

th_mb [   ]

cr_mb [   ]

d_mb [   ]

Name ....

Write the letter pattern ump in each box to make words.

Cover each word and write it from memory.

j [ ] _____

p [ ] _____

b [ ] _____

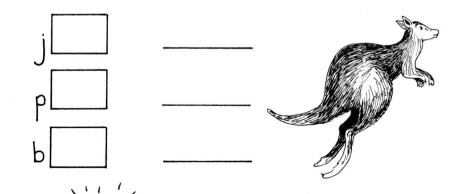

Now ˙burst˙ the words to finish the puzzle.

jumping
|
jumps — jump — jumped
|
jumper

— dump —

— bump —

Name ....

Write the letter pattern ung in each box to make words.

Cover each word and write it from memory.

s[ ] _____   h[ ]ry _____

h[ ] _____

Now sort out these jumbled sentences.

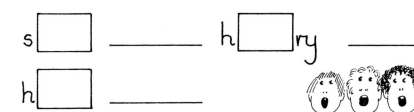

1. children the The concert. at sang

_____

2. was in The picture hall. school hung new the

_____

_____

3. swimming children very After hungry. were the

_____

_____

Name ....

Write the letter pattern unn in each box to make words.

Cover each word and write it from memory.

s[ ]y _____

f[ ]y _____

t[ ]el _____

f[ ]el _____

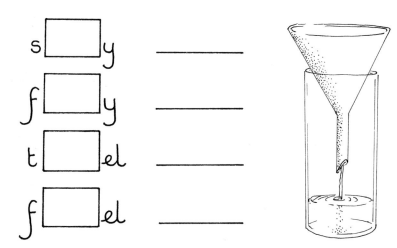

Now use the code to finish the message.

| a = ● | e = ▲ | i = ■ | o = ▼ | u = ◆ |

▼n▲ s◆nny d●y my fr■▲nd ●nd
■ pl●y▲d ■n th▲ t◆nn▲l ●t
th▲ f◆nf●■r.
W▲ cr●wl▲d thr▼◆gh ●nd b◆mp▲d
■nt▼ ▲●ch ▼th▲r.
■t w●s v▲ry f◆nny.

Name ....

Write the letter pattern _ure_ in each box to make words.

Cover each word and write it from memory.

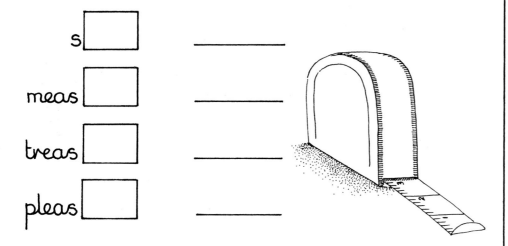

s[   ]   _____

meas[   ]   _____

treas[   ]   _____

pleas[   ]   _____

Now find all the _ure_ words.

curemeasurepurepleasuretreasureleisuresure

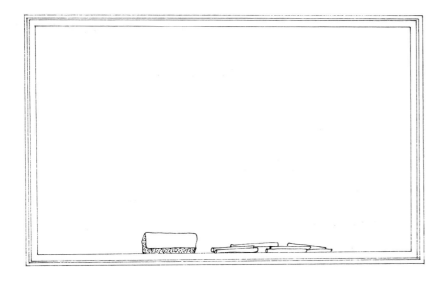

Name ....

Write the word _urn_ in each box to make words.

Cover each word and write it from memory.

t[   ]   _____

b[   ]   _____

ret[   ]   _____

Now read through this story and correct the spelling mistakes.

We made our bonfire from old ferniture, boxes and peices of wood. We took it in turns to throw the rubbish on. It burnt fiercely. Flames crakled and roared. We had to turn our faces away from the heet. The onely thing not to burn was Mum's old cooker.

Name ....

Write the word _use_ in each box to make words.

Cover each word and write it from memory.

☐ ful _____

exc ☐ _____

m ☐ um _____.

ca ☐ _____

beca ☐ _____

Write these words in alphabetical order

Now write what happened on Sunday.

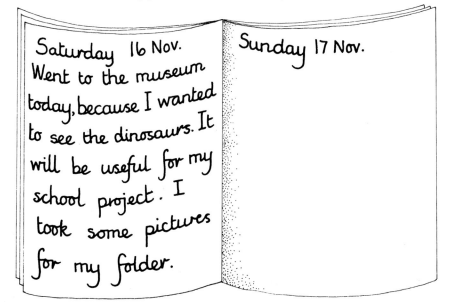

Saturday 16 Nov.
Went to the museum today, because I wanted to see the dinosaurs. It will be useful for my school project. I took some pictures for my folder.

Sunday 17 Nov.

Name ....

Write the letter pattern _ush_ in each box to make words.

Cover each word and write it from memory.

r ☐ _____

cr ☐ _____

thr ☐ _____

br ☐ _____

b ☐ _____

p ☐ _____

Now ⁃ burst ⁃ the words to finish the puzzle.

brushes   brushing
        brush
      brushed

push   crush

Name ....

Write the word *war* in each box to make words.

Cover each word and write it from memory.

☐d	_____
re☐d	_____
☐m	_____
☐ship	_____

Now sort out these jumbled sentences.

1. reward. found I When money the lost a me gave they

_____

_____

2. saw We warship the harbour. the old in.

_____

_____

Name ....

Write the word *win* in each box to make words.

Cover each word and write it from memory.

☐d	_____	t☐s	_____
☐dy	_____	☐g	_____
☐dow	_____	s☐g	_____

Now use some of these words to tell us what the twins saw from the window.

Remember to use capital letters and full stops.

The twins saw _____

_____

_____

_____

Name ....

Write the letter pattern **wor** in each box to make words.

Cover each word and write it from memory.

☐k _____   ☐ld _____

☐d _____   ☐n _____

☐m _____   s☐d _____

Now use some of these words to finish the story.

A brave knight rode the _____ in
search of a dragon. He was _____ out
with searching, as it was very hard
_____ . He couldn't find a dragon
but he did see a _____ wriggling
out of its hole. He took out his
_____ but it was much too
friendly to kill.

Name ....

Write the word **you** in each box to make words.

Cover each word and write it from memory.

☐'ll _____

☐'re _____

☐r _____

☐rself _____

☐ng _____

Who is in the mirror?

_____

_____

Now finish the puzzle.

you will = ☐

you are = ☐

Write the letter pattern *ance* in each box to make words.

Cover each word and write it from memory.

d ☐ _____   dist ☐ _____

ch ☐ _____   entr ☐ _____

bal ☐ _____

Now finish the pattern.

dance		
	balances	
		glancing
advance		

Now answer the questions.

The opposite of retreat is _____ .

The opposite of exit is _____ .

70

Write the letter pattern *ange* in each box to make words.

Cover each word and write it from memory.

ch ☐ _____   str ☐ _____

d ☐ r _____   or ☐ _____

Now use some of these words to finish the crossing code.

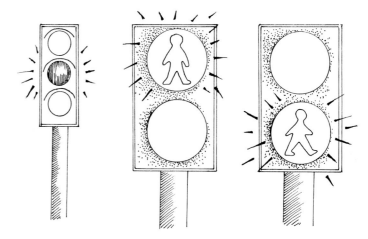

1. Red means stop.

2. Before you cross wait for the lights to _____ .

3. Green means, 'Cross Safely'.

4. _____ means, 'Be careful, traffic moving'.

Name ....

Write the letter pattern atch in each box to make words.

Cover each word and write it from memory.

c ☐ _____

m ☐ _____

w ☐ _____

Now ☼burst☼ the words to finish the puzzle.

matched

matches — match — matching

— watch —

— patch —

— snatch —

Name ....

Write the letter pattern augh in each box to make words.

Cover each word and write it from memory.

l ☐ _____

l ☐ ter _____

c ☐ t _____

t ☐ t _____

d ☐ ter _____

n ☐ ty _____

Now use some of these words to finish the puzzles.

Today I will catch the ball.
Yesterday I ☐ the ball.

Today I will teach the class.
Yesterday I ☐ the class.

Write the word *ball* in each box to make words.

Cover each word and write it from memory.

☐oon _____

foot☐ _____

snow☐ _____

Now finish the diary of your games for the week.

Monday
Burst the _____ at
my party.
Tuesday
Played goalkeeper in
the school _____ team.
Wednesday
Threw a _____
at my friend.

Thursday

Friday

Saturday

Sunday

Write the word *body* in each box to make words.

Cover each word and write it from memory.

any☐ _____

no☐ _____

some☐ _____

every☐ _____

Now help the body builder to find the *body* words.

some   every

any   body   no

Name ....

Write the word **cent** in each box to make words.

Cover each word and write it from memory.

☐ re	_____	
☐ ral	_____	
☐ ury	_____	

How do you reach the prize?

1. Begin at start.
2. Turn _____ .
3. Turn _____ .
4. Turn _____ again.
5. The prize is in the _____ .

Start

What is the prize? ☐

Name ....

Write the letter pattern **circ** in each box to make words.

Cover each word and write it from memory.

☐ le	_____	
☐ ular	_____	
☐ us	_____	

Now use some of these words to tell your friend about your visit to the circus.

Remember to use capital letters and full stops.

At the _____

_____

_____

_____

_____

_____

Name ....

Write the word dent in each box to make words.

Cover each word and write it from memory.

☐ist _____

☐al _____

acci☐ _____

Now use these words to tell your friend what happened.

Our car was in an _____ on the way to the _____. The lights were smashed and the bumper was broken.
When we got to the car park I was too late for my _____ appointment.

Name ....

Write the word each in each box to make words.

Cover each word and write it from memory.

b☐ _____

r☐ _____

t☐ _____

t☐er _____

Now use some of the words to label the pictures.

© LDA A Hand for Spelling Activity Book 3

Write the word *east* in each box to make words.

Cover each word and write it from memory.

b[ ] _____

l[ ] _____

f[ ] _____

[ ]*em* _____

Now print these words to fill the boxes.

Now write out this sentence.

Did you enjoy your Easter egg?

Write the letter pattern *eigh* in each box to make words.

Cover each word and write it from memory.

[ ]t _____

w[ ] _____

w[ ]t _____

n[ ]*bour* _____

h[ ]t _____

Now use some of these words of finish the puzzles.

Someone who lives next door [ ]

The number after seven [ ]

A measure of how tall I am [ ]

A measure of heaviness [ ]

Write the word *even* in each box to make words.

Cover each word and write it from memory.

[ ]ing _____

s[ ] _____

el[ ] _____

Now use some of these words to say what you have
· seen in your garden.

Remember to use capital letters and full stops.

_____

_____

_____

_____

Write the word *ever* in each box to make words.

Cover each word and write it from memory.

n[ ] _____

[ ]y _____

s[ ]al _____

Now find the small words in the following words.

never	every	however

The opposite of always is _____ .

Name ....

Write the word *fact* in each box to make words.

Cover each word and write it from memory.

☐ ory _____

satis ☐ ory _____

manu ☐ ure _____

Now find the small words in the following words.

factory	satisfaction	manufacture

Now write out this sentence.

John's work was very satisfactory.

Name ....

Write the word *hose* in each box to make words.

Cover each word and write it from memory.

t ☐ _____

c ☐ _____

w ☐ _____

Now crack the code to find the words.

a	b	c	d	e	f	g	h	i	j	k	l	m	n	o	p	q	r	s	t	u	v	w	x	y	z
1	2	3	4	5	6	7	8	9	10	11	12	13	14	15	16	17	18	19	20	21	22	23	24	25	26

3 8 15 19 5   _____

23 8 15 19 5   _____

20 8 15 19 5   _____

8 15 19 5   _____

Write the letter pattern *ible* in each box to make words.

Cover each word and write it from memory.

B [ ]   _____

poss [ ]   _____

imposs [ ]   _____

terr [ ]   _____

Now use some of these words to finish the sentences.

1. It was not _____ to climb the hill.

2. It was _____ for me to swim across the ocean.

3. In the _____ wind I lost my umbrella.

Write the letter pattern *ight* in each box to make words.

Cover each word and write it from memory.

n [ ]   _____

m [ ]   _____

s [ ]   _____

f [ ]   _____

stra [ ]   _____   ton [ ]   _____

Write these words in alphabetical order

Now use *ight* words to finish the poem.

Under a street _____

At _____

Two cats _____ ,

Tails stiff and _____

Whiskers bristling,

Catch _____ of a dog

Who runs off in _____ .

Name ....

Write the letter pattern *ince* in each box to make words.

Cover each word and write it from memory.

s [ ] _____

pr [ ] _____

pr [ ] ss _____

s [ ] rely _____

Now use these words to finish the Prince's letter to Cinderella.

The Palace
25 Sept. 1992

Dear Cinderella,
    Ever _____ I saw you at the
ball and you lost your slipper
I've wanted you to be my
_____. Will you marry me?
        Yours _____
        _____ Charming

Name ....

Write the word *king* in each box to make words.

Cover each word and write it from memory.

ma [ ] _____

ta [ ] _____

ba [ ] _____

stoc [ ] _____

as [ ] _____

Write these words in alphabetical order

Now finish the pattern.

make		
	takes	
		baking
	shakes	
wake		

Name ....

Write the word *lies* in each box to make words.

Cover each word and write it from memory.

f[ ] _____

rep[ ] _____

fami[ ] _____

jel[ ] _____

jelly

Now use some of these words to finish the puzzles.

1. They wobble. [ ]

2. These insects buzz about [ ]

3. People who live in houses. [ ]

4. These are not true [ ]

Name ....

Write the letter pattern *ment* in each box to make words.

Cover each word and write it from memory.

mo[ ] _____

ce[ ] _____

govern[ ] _____

Now read through this story and correct the spelling mistakes. Then finish the story.

The puppy jumped over the side of his bocks and ran into the garden where Dad was makeing a path. The sement hadn't set and in a moment he stept in it and left a trial of paw prints. Dad _____ _____

Write the letter pattern **oose** in each box to make words.

Cover each word and write it from memory.

g [ ] _____

l [ ] _____

ch [ ] _____

How many **oose** words can you find in the word search?

s	h	g	l	a	d	e
a	l	o	o	s	e	d
o	o	e	l	d	o	e
c	h	o	o	s	e	m
d	e	g	o	o	s	e
m	o	o	s	e	d	f

The opposite of tight is _____

Write the letter pattern **orry** in each box to make words.

Cover each word and write it from memory.

s [ ] _____

l [ ] _____

w [ ] _____

Now use these words to finish the dictionary list.

_____ a truck to carry heavy goods

_____ to be sad

_____ to be upset

Now write out this sentence.

He was sorry to cause so much worry.

Write the word *other* in each box to make words.

Cover each word and write it from memory.

m[ ] _____

br[ ] _____

an[ ] _____

b[ ] _____

Now find the small words in the following words.

mother	brother	another

Write the letter pattern *ough* in each box to make words.

Cover each word and write it from memory.

c[ ] _____

r[ ] _____

en[ ] _____

th[ ] _____

pl[ ] _____

thr[ ] _____

Now write a sentence which includes each pair of words.

1. cough   sweet _____

_____

2. plough   horses _____

_____

3. through   fence _____

_____

Write the letter pattern **ould** in each box to make words.

Cover each word and write it from memory.

c[ ]n't _____

w[ ]n't _____

sh[ ]n't _____

sh[ ]er _____

b[ ]er _____

m[ ] _____

Now use some of these words to finish the puzzles.

1. What is she trying to push over the cliff? [ ]

2. What part of the body is she using? [ ]

Write the letter pattern **ound** in each box to make words.

Cover each word and write it from memory.

s[ ] _____

m[ ] _____

f[ ] _____

w[ ] _____

Write these words in alphabetical order

Now finish the story using some of these words. Remember to use capital letters and full stops.

The castle stood on a very large _____. As I looked out I heard a very strange _____. It wasn't quite a hiss, it wasn't quite a roar. I waited and then _____

_____

Write the letter pattern **ount** in each box to make words.

Cover each word and write it from memory.

c [ ] _____

m [ ] _____

m [ ] ain _____

am [ ] _____

c [ ] ry _____

Now sort out these jumbled sentences.

1. had a in They holiday country. the

_____

2. all mountain. It day climb to took the

_____

3. can one I count hundred. to

_____

Write the word **port** in each box to make words.

Cover each word and write it from memory.

s [ ] _____

re [ ] _____

air [ ] _____

im [ ] ant _____

Now write these words on the alphabet snake.

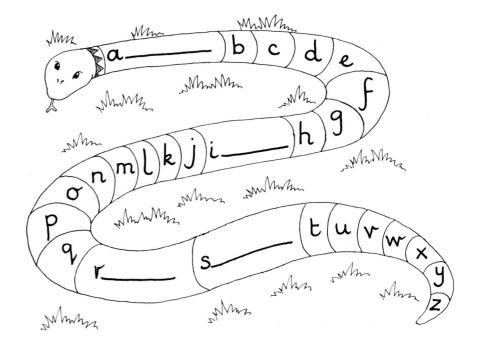

© **LDA** A Hand for Spelling Activity Book 3

Name ....

Write the word *read* in each box to make words.

Cover each word and write it from memory.

☐ y   _____

al ☐ y   _____

b ☐   _____

th ☐   _____

sp ☐   _____

Write these words in alphabetical order

Now use some of the words to make a sandwich.

1. Take a _____ loaf.

2. _____

3. _____

4. _____

Name ....

Write the word *ream* in each box to make words.

Cover each word and write it from memory.

d ☐   _____

st ☐   _____

c ☐   _____

ice - c ☐   _____

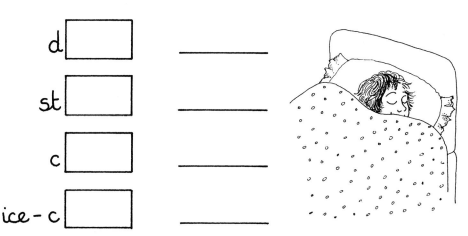

Now match the following words with a picture.

ice - cream

stream

dream

cream

Name ....

Write the word *ring* in each box to make words.

Cover each word and write it from memory.

st [ ] _____

sp [ ] _____

b [ ] _____

b [ ] ing _____

du [ ] _____

Now print these words to fill the boxes.

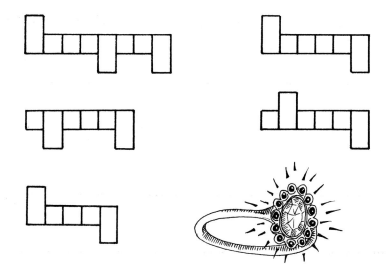

Name ....

Write the letter pattern *rown* in each box to make words.

Cover each word and write it from memory.

c [ ] _____

b [ ] _____

d [ ] _____

g [ ] _____

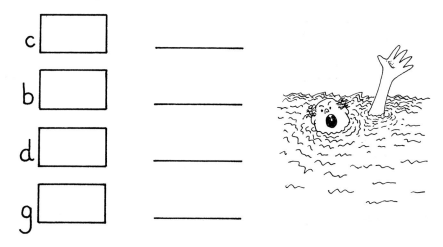

Now write these words on the alphabet trail.

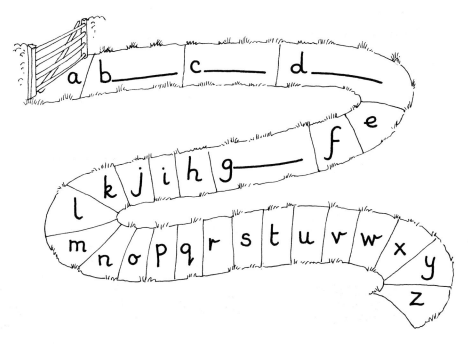

Write the word *rush* in each box to make words.

Cover each word and write it from memory.

c [ ]   _____

b [ ]   _____

th [ ]   _____

Now use *rush* words to finish the crossword.

Across

2. Hurry

3. You sweep with this

4. Squash

Down

1. A garden bird

Write the word *sand* in each box to make words.

Cover each word and write it from memory.

[ ] y   _____

[ ] als   _____

thou [ ]   _____

Which *sand* word does this funny saying spell?

two huge orange umbrellas sat and nattered dreamily [ ]

Can you think of funny sayings for sandy and sandals?

_____

_____

_____

_____

Write the word *self* in each box to make words.

Cover each word and write it from memory.

her ☐ _____

him ☐ _____

my ☐ _____

it ☐ _____

your ☐ _____

Now finish the pattern.

her	
	himself
it	
	myself
your	

Write the word *sent* in each box to make words.

Cover each word and write it from memory.

☐ ence _____

pre ☐ _____

ab ☐ _____

Which *sent* word does this funny saying spell?

six elderly neighbours talking endless nonsense came early

Can you think of funny sayings for present and absent?

_____

_____

_____

_____

Name ....

Write the letter pattern *stor* in each box to make words.

Cover each word and write it from memory.

☐ e _____

☐ y _____

☐ ies _____

☐ m _____

☐ k _____

Now find all the *stor* words.

stormstoriesstorestorkstory

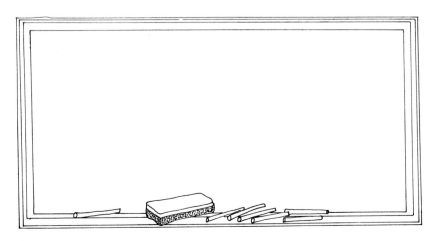

Name ....

Write the letter pattern *ture* in each box to make words.

Cover each word and write it from memory.

cap ☐ _____

pic ☐ _____

punc ☐ _____

manufac ☐ _____

Now match the following words with a picture.

picture

puncture

manufacture

capture

Name ....

Write the word **aught** in each box to make words.

Cover each word and write it from memory.

c[ ] _____

t[ ] _____

n[ ] _____

n[ ]y _____

d[ ]er _____

l[ ]er _____

Now use some of these words to finish the rhyme.

One teacher _____

Two _____ pupils

Who _____

Three rabbits

Chasing all round the classroom.

Name ....

Write the word **ought** in each box to make words.

Cover each word and write it from memory.

n[ ] _____

b[ ] _____

f[ ] _____

th[ ] _____

br[ ] _____

dr[ ] _____

Now finish the pattern.

buy	
	fought
think	
bring	

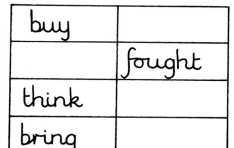

_____ means having no water.

Name ....

Write the letter pattern   in each box to make words.

Cover each word and write it from memory.

Name ....

Write the letter pattern   in each box to make words.

Cover each word and write it from memory.

Name ....

Write the word   in each box to make words.

Cover each word and write it from memory.

☐   _____

☐   _____

☐   _____

☐   _____

Name ....

Write the word   in each box to make words.

Cover each word and write it from memory.

☐   _____

☐   _____

☐   _____

☐   _____

© LDA A Hand for Spelling Activity Book 3